SELLING SKILLS

SELF-STUDY SERIES

SC SHORE
CONSULTING

ABOUT THE AUTHOR

Jeff Shore is a highly sought-after sales keynote speaker, author and consultant. For more than three decades, Jeff has guided sales executives and sales teams in large and small companies across the globe to deliver profitable customer-first sales results.

In a crowded field of sales keynote speakers and sales training programs, Jeff Shore stands out with his research-based "buying formula" methodology. Combining his extensive front-line sales experience with the latest leading-edge research into buyer psychology, Jeff has created a highly effective, personalized way to reset sales paradigms and deliver industry-leading results.

Jeff holds the prestigious Certified Speaking Professional designation from the National Speakers Association (NSA) and is a member of the NSA's exclusive Million Dollar Speakers Group. Jeff tailors every keynote to your business and your team while electrifying your audience through captivating real-world case studies, inspiring personal stories, hard-working and straightforward sales strategies, and his engaging trademark humor.

Jeff won't just teach you how to sell…he'll show you how to change your mindset AND how to change your world.

jeffshore.com
jeff@jeffshore.com
(844) 54-SHORE

MAXIMIZE!

**8 Daily Habits
for Getting *MORE* Than
Your Fair Share
in *ANY* Market**

BY JEFF SHORE

ISBN: 978-0-9884915-6-4

Cover and page design by Kista Cook.

Shore Consulting books are available at special quantity discounts to use as premiums and sales promotions or for use in corporate training programs. To contact a representative, please visit the Contact page at www.jeffshore.com or call +1 844-54-SHORE.

CONTENTS

INTRODUCTION

You are reading this book because you want to develop a *Maximize!* mindset, yes? And you can get that mindset in a book, right? Uh...nope.

News flash: You don't need to read a book with 50,000 words and 200-plus pages to get your head straight. Such a book would not do the trick. A book is simply an inanimate object that demands absolutely nothing of you.

So what makes for a *Maximize!* mindset? It's not the words you read on the pages of a book; it is the response that is demonstrated by your actions.

This short book was not written as an exhaustive psychological tome that explains the inner workings of the motivated brain. Nor is it intended to be a feel-good, motivational shot in the arm.

This book was written to inspire action.

I wrote this book with sales professionals in mind, but the principles will apply to anyone. That is, the principles will apply if the principles are *applied!*

That action starts with mindset, but the mental approach

is useless until concrete steps are taken.

So as you read through this book, do so with a pen in hand. Write down not only your insights, but also your commitments. Build in a bias for action. Expect that you will do things differently after each short chapter.

I want you to *Maximize!* the opportunities in front of you every day. I want you to *Maximize!* your mindset. I want you to *Maximize!* your actions.

Mostly, I want to see you *Maximize!* your success!

Jeff Shore

MAXIMIZE!

Get Fired Up!

CHAPTER 1

CHAPTER 1:

Get Fired Up!

Think of the most successful people you've ever known. Or those you have read about over the years. Think about Jeff Bezos and Serena Williams. About Sarah Blakely and Patrick Mahomes. Think about any of the regulars on *Shark Tank*.

What do they have in common? In one word: passion.

So many sales professionals dream of success, but their passion is limited to their dreams. When you think about uber-successful people you'll notice something important. Their passion does not end with their dreams; it carries through to their execution.

Is that true for you?

True sales success is absolutely dependent on one's passion to execute well. Whether you're thinking about undertaking a program, a process, or an initiative of any kind, or if you just want a better sales presentation, you need to possess enough passion to carry you through to its perfect completion.

That passion I'm speaking about is more than a passing phase. It's not something I get from a seminar or a motivational speech. I can get temporarily fired up in such ways, but true passion is lasting passion.

Stop for a moment and ask yourself the question, "What am I deeply passionate about?" I'm talking about a motivating force that is deep within your soul. It cannot be manufactured or faked. But it can be expanded, and that is our focus here.

Passion is the secret weapon. Passion is the fuel that carries us to places we cannot otherwise reach.

But passion is not simply enthusiasm. Enthusiasm is typically temporary and based upon circumstances. I can be enthusiastic based on external forces, but such an emotion rarely lasts all that long. Passion is internal and consistent over time.

If I lack passion for true sales excellence, what is likely to happen? I might begin my day with a degree of enthusiasm, perhaps even a great deal of enthusiasm. But as the day churns on, my lack of passion will begin to surface and my enthusiasm will wane. I may have been "gung ho" at the start of the day, but I simply don't have enough passion to carry it through to the end. My presentations slip as the day goes on. Eventually, I'm just going through the motions.

Let me share an example from my personal experience. My wife and I have been in our home for several years now but I still have boxes that I haven't unpacked. (Show of hands for those of you in the same boat?) I tell myself these boxes are not that important but, from time to time, it annoys me that they're still there, reminding me that the job is still not complete.

Why haven't I unpacked? It's pretty simple. I don't have the passion. If I had the necessary passion, I'd be inspired to act and those boxes would be gone. The lesson? Passion drives us forward, even when our energy is low.

Here is another example—but this time from a positive perspective. When I think about writing a book (and I try to write one book a year) I get extremely passionate about the project. And because I have a high level of passion, when I get writer's block, when I get stumped, when I get stuck in the mire of the writing process, my passion drives me to keep writing—to carry on until the book is finished.

Think back on your own career or aspects of your personal life. Can you recall a time when your passion carried you through even when your enthusiasm waned? That's the difference—passion wins out in the end.

But now let's look at your career endeavors. How passionate are you about perfecting your own sales presentation? Answer with your actions, please. Show me; don't tell me.

The key question we need to ask ourselves: "How do we develop passion?"

I suggest the best way to develop passion is to carefully consider the benefits of an initiative's outcomes—*before you even start*. If you begin a project (a sales performance improvement project, for example) by thinking about its value in the end, you will cultivate the passion needed to carry it through to its completion.

Say, for example, that you want to master the subject of buyer financing so that you can be the go-to expert in helping more people to purchase. On the surface, the idea of studying financing and developing a more robust presentation might not sound all that appealing; your enthusiasm might be low.

But if you stop to consider the value you can bring to your customers and to the number of lives you can impact in undertaking such a development program, your passion increases and the actions follow thereafter.

My challenge for you

Think about a project, a program, or a process you want to work on right now. Then ask yourself, "What end goal would motivate me to remain passionate all the way through to completion?"

That vision clarity is critical right out of the gate. Vision clarity gives us focus, direction, and the basic framework for a strategy.

When we clarify our goals and establish the value of completing a project at the *beginning*, our passion will follow. The rest of the steps become relatively easy.

Follow. Your. Passion. And let your passion carry you through to success.

SELF-STUDY QUESTIONS:

1. *Think of a goal, large or small, that has been on your mind for some time. Write down and clarify the end result of the goal. What will it look like and feel like when the goal is achieved?*

2. *Identify one aspect of your sales presentation that could use some work. What will your performance look like when you have perfected that aspect of your presentation?*

3. *This week, do a passion gut check. What motivates you? What inspires you? What do you find so interesting and exciting that you could do it for a very long time? Write your answers down so that they are concrete instead of abstract.*

MAXIMIZE!

Engage!

CHAPTER 2:

· ·

Engage!

Ever hear (or say) these words? "I want my fair share!"

Not me…I want *more* than my fair share. I want my fair share, and then I want someone else's fair share as well.

If you're in sales, I hope you feel the same way.

I understand that this might sound arrogant. But *why* do I want more than my fair share? I'll tell you why. Because if I perform at a higher level, I *earn* more than my fair share.

There is an argument that the New England Patriots won more than their fair share of Super Bowl titles during their dynasty. How did they do that? They *earned* it. They outworked, outhustled, outperformed everyone else.

So how do you earn more than your fair share? It begins with a critically important concept: FULL ENGAGEMENT.

If you want to really stand out, it starts by being 100% focused on executing your plan for success. You need to be so fully present in your endeavor that you achieve total concentration on the objective in front of you.

Some call it "the zone," that place where your focus is so intense that the rest of the world fades away. There are no mental distractions in the zone. Only full engagement.

Want an example? Elite professional tennis players share a common physical attribute: Their heart rate goes down between points. When they are not actually playing a point they allow themselves to mentally relax. Why? So that when they play again they are so completely in the full engagement zone that they become unbeatable. Lesser players find a consistent heart rate throughout the match, but they never reach that zone moment.

Full engagement is the idea of being completely absorbed. For sales professionals, that means being locked in on developing and practicing your perfect sales presentation. This is a rarity, in my own personal observation. The majority of salespeople I have observed approach training and development with caution and reservation. They refuse to fully commit; they hold back. They never get to full engagement because something holds them back: ego, pride, embarrassment, comfort addictions—whatever it may be.

If you want to get more than your fair share of sales, it means your customer needs to see that you are more vested, more present, more prepared, and more engaged than any other salesperson they've ever dealt with.

Customers are drawn in by this. They appreciate that emotional relationship. Great salespeople look for that opportunity of connecting right from the very beginning.

We can look at technique all day long, and well we should. But being in that total concentration zone is about having the technique down so well that we aren't even thinking about our sales presentation. Instead, we are zoned in on the person standing in front of us.

My wife and I were in Hawaii recently and we went to dinner at the Lahaina Grill. I have to tell you, the hostess was amazing.

She came out from behind the stand, she greeted us warmly, and she introduced herself. She made it seem like she was personally holding a party, and that Karen and I were the guests of honor. She remembered our names throughout the evening and even as we were leaving she said, "Jeff, Karen, was your dinner experience all that you hoped for?" It was amazing!

What made our experience so memorable? *Full engagement—* the fact that the hostess was emotionally connected with us throughout the experience.

Now that's just a dining experience that lasts only a couple of hours. How much more important is full engagement in a buyer-seller relationship?

Can you picture a time when you were shopping for something (a car, shoes, golf clubs) and the salesperson was only partially engaged? You know the exact experience I'm referring to, don't you?

Conversely, can you recall an experience where a sales professional was demonstrating total concentration on you and your needs? They were in a zone, and you could feel it.

This is what great salespeople do. They eliminate mental distractions. They're not thinking about what they need to do next. They are so fully focused on their customer that the customer senses that they are being served. Not sold to...but *served*.

When we show our customers total concentration we have the opportunity of making an impression that no other salesperson can make.

We maximize the customer's experience by being fully engaged. We perform at a higher level by being fully engaged. And by being fully engaged, we *earn* more than our fair share.

My challenge for you

What can you do to ensure you are flexing your "total engagement" muscle? I encourage you to get out of your comfort zone and start by doing the following this week:

1. Eliminate all distractions and commit to 100% concentration with your next three prospects.

2. After each encounter take some time to jot down how you felt. Take note of the things that attempted to distract you and how you handled each distraction.

3. Practice full engagement in other areas of your life. Work on total concentration in your conversations with family and friends. This isn't just a good sales skill; it is a powerful life skill!

SELF-STUDY QUESTIONS:

1. *Think about an experience you had with a salesperson who was not fully engaged. How did that make you feel? What was distracting about the interaction? What could the salesperson have done differently?*

2. *What can you do to mentally prepare yourself to be fully engaged with your customers? To ensure that you are in "the zone"?*

3. *At the end of this week, take a few minutes to evaluate your interactions and conversations with your customers. Were you fully engaged with every customer? What could you have done differently to ensure you were fully serving your customers' needs?*

MAXIMIZE!

Get 'Er Done!

CHAPTER 3:

Get 'Er Done!

Think back to the last time you went on vacation. Specifically, think back to the day before you left. Even more specifically, think about the last two hours before you shut it all down.

Question: How much do you get done in the last two hours before you leave on vacation?

I see vacation as a reward for all the time I put into my busy career. I love my work, but I also love the breaks. I *need* the breaks. I find that resting my brain is a powerful way to refresh my creativity. Stepping away is an important means of renewal.

So why do I get so much done in the two hours before a vacation? Because I don't want to take any undone work with me!

Of course, there's much to be done in those final two hours. Ironically, because you're motivated to perform at such a high level—because the goal is to free your mind and truly enjoy the time off—you'll find that those two hours are extremely productive.

I don't know about you, but in those last few work hours before vacation I am a production machine. I mean seriously—I can crank out tasks like nobody's business.

What can you learn from this situation? If you want to boost your productivity, you can begin with a little trick that I call "the two-hour workday."

What if you embraced a mindset where you only had two hours to get everything done in your workday? What would those two hours look like?

I'll tell you what they would look like. You would get rid of all distractions. You would put your head down and pound away. You would power through a tremendous amount of work.

Now, imagine if you started every normal workday in that fashion. Imagine if you looked at your day and said, "I want to get so much done in my first two hours that it feels like I've completed an entire day's worth of work." At that point, the rest of the day seems like bonus time that enhances your productivity.

Of course, it's not just pounding out tasks. It's about pounding out the tasks that really matter.

Here's a tip I learned from entrepreneurial coach Dan Sullivan. Don't start your day with twenty-eight things on your to-do list; just work on the three things that will really matter and get them done right away.

How does that help? Well, if I have twenty-eight things on my list and I only accomplish twelve, how do I feel at the end of the day? Like a failure, right?

But if I have just three very important things on my list and I accomplish seven, how do I feel? Like an overachiever!

Don't lose the game when you are the one writing the rules!!!

So what really matters to you? And what matters most? These are critically important questions because they allow you to measure your activities against what has the greatest impact.

Stephen Covey wrote, "The main thing is to keep the main thing the main thing." Alas, far too many people have never really settled in on identifying that main thing.

But I know!

If you're in sales I can tell you one thing that should ALWAYS be at the top of your list—your main thing: *lead conversion!* There is no simpler or more accurate way to define your job in two words.

You can and should begin every day with what I call the "Lead Conversion Hour." A full hour—early in the day—dedicated to moving prospects along in the sales funnel. Honing in on this "main thing" opportunity early in the day will provide a significant return on your time investment. You'll write more sales, make more money, and feel far more accomplished if you get your Lead Conversion Hour accomplished first thing in the day.

How great would you feel if you had a solid hour of lead conversion time under your belt by 10 a.m.? What a rush!

If you want to leave your workday feeling fulfilled and satisfied, pack your most important work into the front of the day. You will immediately notice a substantial productivity boost. You will see your stress reduced. You will see your performance increase. And you will be a much more effective sales professional.

My challenge for you

I encourage you to start your day focusing on what *really* matters, start by doing the following this week:

1. Think about everything you have on your to-do list. Now select three things that matter the most. Schedule these things into your day first thing tomorrow morning. Make it a challenge to get them done early.

2. Take note of how you feel when you've accomplished the three tasks (or more) that matter the most in the first two hours of your workday. Leverage that momentum going forward.

3. Initiate a Lead Conversion Hour right away. Put it down in your calendar and get into that early-in-the-day rhythm.

SELF-STUDY QUESTIONS:

1. *What habits do you have that could be preventing (or distracting) you from accomplishing the tasks that are most important early in your workday? What can you do differently to ensure you're accomplishing the most important tasks each day?*

2. *If you embraced the mindset that you had two hours to get everything done in your workday, what would be the most important tasks to accomplish? How would you ensure you got the tasks accomplished in the two hours?*

3. *This week, get your lead conversion done early, put it on your calendar each day (remember to make it early in the day), and stay committed to it! Reflect back on the week when it's done. How does it feel to have an hour each day committed to just lead conversion?*

MAXIMIZE!

Take Action!

CHAPTER 4

CHAPTER 4:
. . . .
Take Action!

Do you want to learn to execute properly? Here's an idea. Stop focusing on the results!

You read that right; stop focusing on the results. I know it sounds counterintuitive, but hear me out. In sales, we have a tendency to get so hung up on results that we forget to pay attention to the behaviors that produce the results.

I play ice hockey (or as they call it in Canada, "hockey"). Because I play in the defenseman position, I understand an important principle: The other team cannot score if the puck never gets to the net. Consequently, when I'm on the ice I never think about the scoreboard. I only think about one thing: blocking shots.

The scoreboard shows the result, but it does not show the behavior that leads to the result. Specific individual actions will eventually add up to the numbers on the board.

You must understand this truth: A sale is *not* a behavior. Rather, it is a result of the right behaviors.

Every now and then I come across a salesperson who displays some really poor behaviors yet still garners successful results. Typically what I find is that it is the market that is bringing in these sales rather than superb sales behaviors.

But that situation is an anomaly. The salesperson simply has the right product, at the right time, in the right market conditions, with the right buyer. The sale just happens.

Would you want to be dependent upon perfect-case scenarios for your success? I think not!

Conversely, I have seen the opposite happen. Salespeople who are pushing all the right buttons, who are doing everything they're supposed to do, but are not getting the results. If we only look at results, we would judge these salespeople failures.

This is a big mistake. It actually falls under the definition of what psychologists refer to as the "hindsight bias." Basically, we determine whether the behaviors were appropriate only by looking at the end result.

They say that hindsight is 20/20, but that is not entirely accurate. There are times when we look at the end result and believe we understand how we got there. But what if our vision is faulty?

For example, when the stock market crashed in 2008 there were people who said they *knew* it was going to happen. Michael Lewis's book *The Big Short* chronicles the actions of people who could see what was about to go down. They *knew* the outcome before it took place, right?

In reality, and according to Nobel-prize-winning psychologist Daniel Kahneman, they didn't really *know* it was going to happen. They merely *thought* they knew it was going to happen. At that same time, there were equally intelligent people with access to the exact same information who did not believe a crash was imminent. Based on the end result, we are inclined to believe that those who "predicted" the crash had the right behaviors.

From a sales perspective, consider a salesperson working with a prospect who is closing in on a purchase decision. At the moment of truth, the salesperson decides *not* to ask a closing question. The justification (and I've heard this one before): "She'll let me know when she's ready to buy." In this situation, the customer has a glaring need and the product checks all the boxes. The customer blurts out, "I'll take it."

How does the salesperson react? With a self-affirmation that NOT asking for the sale was the right thing to do. After all, the strategy was successful, was it not?

This is a prime example of the hindsight bias in action, and it is devastating. Because in this instance it will reinforce poor behavior and lead the salesperson to follow the same course of (non) action in the future.

The question we need to ask ourselves in evaluating effective execution is this: "What can we control in the sales process?"

The fact of the matter is, we cannot control the results, but we can always control the behavior.

Again, we have a salesperson who declined to ask the closing question. So who was in control of the process at that point—the salesperson or the buyer? The buyer!

Just because the behavior led to the desired result doesn't make the behavior correct. As a golf instructor once told me, "Just because the ball went straight doesn't mean you hit it properly."

If you want to promote effective execution dependably and consistently, you must pay attention to the core success behaviors. You must focus on the specific actions that repeatedly produce positive sales results.

When we put too much emphasis on the end result, we tend to reward haphazardness at the expense of effective execution.

The takeaway? If you want to evaluate your own sales performance or the performance of the people around you, start using metrics that are based on behaviors. Measure the value of steps being taken during the process rather than fixating on results.

If the behaviors are right, the results will be positive more often than not. Effective execution is found in the building blocks of right behaviors. Get those right and successful results will follow.

My challenge for you

Start evaluating your behaviors throughout the sales cycle with your customers. Are they the right behaviors to get the results you desire? Work on your execution this week by doing the following:

1. Think about your sales process and write down four to six critical behaviors. These are specific actions or phrases that help determine success.

2. In your sales presentations this week, work on nailing each of those four to six critical behaviors you identified. Total concentration. Execute perfectly.

3. Consider reading John Wooden's excellent book, *Wooden on Leadership*. Wooden was the master of coaching for behaviors rather than coaching for results.

SELF-STUDY QUESTIONS:

1. *Besides not asking for the sale, what are some examples of faulty sales behaviors that could still show positive results?*

2. *What is it about the scoreboard that is so appealing to us? Why do we tend to look at the scoreboard more than the behaviors?*

3. *This week, take some time after each interaction with a customer to reflect and review your actions. Write down a few behaviors you could improve from those interactions and identify what you can work on to improve your behaviors in the future.*

MAXIMIZE!

Exceed!

CHAPTER 5:

Exceed!

My son Kevin has a theater arts background. One of the things that always impressed me about Kevin was that when he was in a show, he always had his lines memorized much earlier than was required. The director would tell the cast to have their lines committed to memory—or what they call "being off script"—by a certain date. Kevin *always* had it done much earlier.

Why? Because Kevin knew that the sooner he got his lines memorized, the more he could truly *act*. He didn't have to think about his lines. He could focus on the moment.

I get tons of Facebook greetings on my birthday; you probably do as well. Overachievers actually send me a text message. But my friend Mike Lyon sends me a video greeting. Every year without fail, Mike takes a few seconds to record a birthday message.

Take a guess how many Facebook greetings I can recall after they are sent? Not many. But a video from Mike Lyon—that's memorable.

These are examples of what I call a "+1 mentality." It begins with a question: "What is expected of me?" But there is an opportunity to take one more additional step. It begins with the requirement, but what is the requirement...*plus one*?

If you want to boost your sales productivity, the +1 mentality is a great way to accomplish that goal.

The world is full of people who are willing to do a mediocre level of work—just good enough to get by. We don't need more of these underachievers.

It's no different in the world of sales. The sales universe is already full of sales practitioners who are trying to figure out how to put out the least amount of effort and still get the job done.

There is a psychological basis to this referred to by researcher Daniel Kahneman as "the law of least effort." Khaneman suggests that the brain is an incredible energy-saving machine; it's always looking for how to accomplish a task with a minimum amount of exertion.

In management circles we call this efficiency. For salespeople we call it laziness!

If you truly want to maximize, you need to realize that your brain will actually hold you back if you let it. Your brain will send a signal in the form of two very dangerous words: "good enough." As in, "That amount of practice was good enough." Or, "My closing technique is good enough." Or perhaps, "When it comes to follow-up, e-mails are good enough."

The fact is that you need to override your own brain in order to truly maximize your effort.

As a successful sales professional, as someone who wants to make a huge impact, who wants to be more than successful, you need to adopt the +1 mentality.

Let's say, for example, that you're selling homes and a client has asked you for information about the local schools. You can go online and e-mail a few links to test scores and programs—that would be "good enough." Or you can pick up the phone and call the principal! Ask her if you could ask her some questions about her school. Let her know that you are constantly talking to potential new residents in her school's zone and it would be very helpful to hear some of the reasons why the school is a good school and what improvements they are planning for the future.

Suppose you're selling high-end stereo systems and a customer asks you about sound quality. You can go on the manufacturer's website and find a glossy brochure that promises incredible tones. Or you can get a video testimonial from a past customer who bought the same system and is ecstatic.

What does +1 look like for you?

In fact, I'm going to suggest that right after you finish reading this chapter, you sit down and write out the sales activities you have right in front of you today: e-mails, phone calls, face-to-face conversations, updates to your clients, referral requests, etc. List everything you need to get done today.

Now ask yourself, "How can I +1 every single one of those activities? What would be one additional step I can add to each of these activities?"

Really give that some thought. What you will end up with is your list of regular activities in one column and your list of +1 activities in an adjacent column. Adding all those small extra steps to your daily activities will create a huge impact.

Everybody else typically calls it quits when things get challenging. To them, mediocre is enough. But you're going to rise above your competitors because you're ready to do things that most others are simply not willing to do. You're committed to taking one step more to achieve excellence in your profession.

So, if you want to boost your sales productivity, +1 everything that you do. Be specific. Be intentional. Be determined. When you do, you'll put yourself on the fast track to maximizing your success as a sales professional.

My challenge for you

What can you do to embrace the +1 mentality? I encourage you to step up your efforts. Start by doing the following this week:

1. Take a piece of paper and draw a line down the middle. On the left side, write a list of several sales activities that you would perform in the course of a day. On the right side, write down a +1 idea that would take that activity to the next level.

2. Use several of your +1 ideas with your customers and journal your results as you do. Share your successes with others.

SELF-STUDY QUESTIONS:

1. *Think about an experience you have had with a salesperson where you didn't feel like they were fully committed to helping you. What could the salesperson have done to make the experience more engaging for you? How could they have served you to the best of their ability?*

2. *Brainstorm some ideas you can utilize to go the extra mile for your customers. How can you stand out and rise above your competitors when engaging with your customers?*

3. *At the end of this week, take a few minutes to evaluate the +1 activities that you implemented. What was the reaction from your customers? Were you able to keep the sale moving forward because of your added effort?*

MAXIMIZE!

Close!

CHAPTER 6:

. . . .

Close!

If you're in sales and you truly want to maximize, you MUST master the art of the ask. Asking a closing question is simply not optional.

But what closing question? How do you do that? How do you maximize the opportunity?

So here it is, the big reveal…the Jeff-Shore-Super-Secret-Final-Knock-'Em-Dead-Scoreboard-Baby Close! Here's what you do: Turn to the customers and give them a smug smile. Wink. Pause for 1.5 seconds, then reach down, hitch up your pants and say, "What's it gonna take to get you to buy my product today?" Emphasize the word "you," and be sure to point at them with both hands (index fingers out, thumbs up, like a couple of guns). Then shut up, because as we have all been taught, the next person who speaks…

If you've studied my stuff in the past you know that this is the polar opposite of anything I would ever espouse!

In fact, I'm afraid you're in for a letdown. Because this isn't rocket science, and there isn't some magic bullet, one-size-fits-all question that will assure you achieve sales success.

The final close is relational. It's an extension of the relationship you have developed with your customer. It's the natural culmination of everything that has happened up to that point. But "natural" does not in any way mean you should "just let it happen."

Asking for the sale is more about intent than it is about technique. What is your mindset in this moment? At the time of the final close are you feeling:

- Joyful?
- Satisfied?
- Confident?
- Serving?
- Proud?

If you're seriously stressed when the voice in your head is telling you to ask for the sale, you're doing it wrong. Asking for the sale must be a time of calm confidence and positive energy. The mindset of a great salesperson is one of satisfaction in helping customers fulfill their mission.

That said, there must be no pause or hesitation when the voice in your head tells you, "It's time." You need an auto-response, a go-to question that you're not making up on the fly. This question should be smooth, natural, simple, and most importantly, relational. And it has to confirm that the customer has agreed to purchase. Craft your go-to question and practice it out loud over and over.

The benefit in the auto-response, for you *and* for your customer, is confidence. You can ask for the sale without any stress on your part, stress that could be transferred to your buyer.

The final close requires mental preparation on your part. It might sound like a strange concept, but you can prepare for this moment by relying on the principles of Cognitive Behavioral Therapy. This popular therapeutic approach to brain training teaches that you can plan and rehearse your mental response in advance of a potentially stressful moment. In other words, you can decide *right now* how you will respond when the voice tells you to ask for the sale. You can decide how you will feel, what you will say, and how you will respond to the customer's answer.

If you decide these things now, before the stress of the closing moment sets in, you will make a choice from the logical side of your brain. If you are unprepared when the voice goes off, you will likely respond from the emotional side of your brain. That part of your brain desires comfort, and it will suggest—strongly—that you back off from asking for the sale.

Be aware of this: Very, *very* few sales are lost because salespeople are too assertive. In those rare cases, the loss happens because the relational foundation is not strong. But you love your customer and they love you right back. Do them a favor—ask them to buy!

My guess is that some of you might be feeling let down right now. You've come to the "Close" section of the book and there are, well, no final closes for you to leverage. Let me offer this suggestion...

Think about how you would ask for the sale from your best friend. However you would do that with him or her, do the same with your customer. Your relationship with your BFF is personal, of course, so the wording will be unique to you. It might sound something like, "You know I wouldn't steer you wrong; I think you should do this." Or perhaps, "I can't make the decision for you, but I think this is the right thing to do. What do you think?" Or with *really* close relationships, "C'mon, ya knucklehead—what are you waiting for!" The point is to be relational when you close.

If you are in sales and you want to truly maximize, this step is not optional. You must MASTER the art of the close. Make it easy for the customer to do what they already want to do. Ask for the sale!

My challenge for you

What can you do to ensure you are *always* asking your customer for the sale? I encourage you to start by doing the following this week:

1. Craft your "go-to" closing question. Practice it out loud several times, and then with a peer once you are feeling confident. And finally with your manager once you have perfected it.

2. Take some time to visualize your sales process and put yourself in the closing moment. Plan for your mental response first and then say the closing question out loud, feeling confident and joyful when you do.

SELF-STUDY QUESTIONS:

1. *Do you ever have negative thoughts at the time of the close? What could you do to change your closing mindset?*

2. *How would you ask your best friend to make a purchase decision? Would you feel comfortable using this question with a customer? If not, rewrite your close until it feels comfortable and confident for you.*

3. *This week, ask every one of your customers for the sale. Don't let them ask you! How did it feel? How did your customers react? Thinking back on the week, would you change how you asked for the sale?*

MAXIMIZE!

Reach!

CHAPTER 7:

. . . .

Reach!

Several years ago I endeavored to utilize the P90X workout program—the really, really (really!) intense fitness and exercise regimen. You may have seen the infomercial. Any Xers out there?

One of the most powerful things I learned from that program is that my brain tends to give out before my body does. My brain gets tired before my body gets tired.

During that experience I learned something important, not just about my workout routine but about life in general. The real magic happens when I take that one extra step.

One more practice repetition. One more round of exercise. One more recital of a good closing technique.

The brain is an energy-conserving machine. The brain recalls very primitive days when we suddenly found ourselves in armed combat or needing to get away from a saber-toothed tiger. The brain encouraged us to conserve energy for when we faced a life-threatening situation.

I wrote about this in Chapter 5: Exceed! You'll recall the discussion about the +1 mentality. That conversation was about adding something to the service to your customer, about exceeding their expectations and thereby standing apart from the crowd.

In this chapter I'm talking about perseverance. About going the extra mile. About not giving up when mediocre salespeople would throw in the towel.

Our brains tells us that we need to conserve our energy as part of our "survival instinct." My friend Dr. Marc Schoen puts it this way: "Your survival instinct is killing you."

When my brain is telling me to shut it down—that enough is enough—I need to choose to keep pushing forward. If I really want to gain great results, I find those results when taking those extra steps in those crucial moments.

Top performers in all walks of life understand that it is the extra effort where the real improvement lies. Talk to Eric Clapton or Michael Jordan or Kendall Coyne Schofield. They will all tell you the same thing. They dominated their areas of expertise because they pressed on when everyone else went home.

It's the same way in sales. One of the questions I constantly ask myself when I'm watching a sales conversation is, "Who stopped the sale?"

There are many times when the customer stops the sale and for all kinds of legitimate reasons. But the sales professional must *never* stop the sale. Salespeople are tasked with taking every sales opportunity as far as it will go.

The best way to make sure you never stop a sale is to constantly ask the question, "Is there one more step I can take?"

You can do this in real time during the sales conversation. But you can also do it by stepping aside after the sales conversation and simply asking yourself, "If there was one more step I could have taken, what would that look like? What could I have done?"

Too many salespeople give up at the first sign of trouble. The customer says, "That's a lot of good information; I need to think about it." The salesperson responds, "I understand. This is a big decision. Give it some thought and call me if you have any questions."

Let me ask you—who is in control of the process at that point? Answer: the customer! Great salespeople are control freaks. They despise the thought of not being in control.

But if we back that up and ask if there is one more step, everything changes. The salesperson could have responded by saying, "I get it; it's a lot of information. But I can only offer this price right here and right now. So let's take a step back and talk about what is clear and what is fuzzy for you. Let's start with what is clear. Tell me what you like about what you've seen."

The strategy here is to keep the sale alive and to do so by rekindling the customer's appreciation for what the future could look like.

Asking about that one next step is a great way to establish self-accountability and to make sure you are not quitting on yourself. Top professionals are always the ones who are willing to put in the extra effort, to go the extra mile, to do the little extra things that mediocre performers are simply not willing to do.

Don't let your comfort addiction get in the way of your success. And by all means do not let your comfort addiction prevent you from best serving your customer's interest!

So, push forward when your brain wants to stop. Go the extra mile. Take that one more step. You'll find that to be the greatest opportunity for growth as a sales professional.

My challenge for you

What can you do to ensure you're taking a sale as far as you can? Go the extra mile this week! Work on taking one more step this week by doing the following:

1. Make the effort to keep that conversation going, even when your comfort-addicted brain tells you to give up.

2. Focus on the concept, "Is there one more step I could take?" with every customer.

SELF-STUDY QUESTIONS:

1. *Think about your last two or three non-sales customers, people who opted not to buy. How did your conversation with them end? Who stopped the sale?*

2. *Now recreate the conversations with those customers and come up with new conclusions. How could you have kept that sale going? What would that creative next step have been?*

3. *This week, keep track of how many times you kept the conversation going. How many times did you take the sale as far as it could go? Be honest! Now reflecting back on the week, were you able to overcome your comfort addictions? How can you continue working on taking the sale as far as it can go?*

. . . .

. . . .

. . . .

. . . .

. . . .

. . . .

. . . .

. . . .

MAXIMIZE!

Celebrate!

CHAPTER 8:

Celebrate!

At age six: "If you clean your room, I'll take you out for ice cream."
At age ten: "If you get good grades this year we'll go to Disneyland."
At age 18: "If you graduate with honors we'll buy you a car."

You know that's the oldest parenting trick in the book. "If you do this, I'll do that…" It's very simple; here is the task and there is the reward.

Why do parents do that? Because it works. We are wired for achievement. When these specific actions lead to those specific rewards, we will work hard to get there.

We apply this in our parenting style, so why don't we apply this concept to our own execution? Is it possible to use that same technique…on yourself?

It is!

Stephen Covey offers the advice that we should always "begin with the end in mind." In sales, we tend to think that "the end" is getting the sale. It's the "yes" from the customer. It's the rush of putting a deal together.

But I would contend that the end of the sale is not the close; it's the celebration that follows!

Too many times we plan out the steps of a process (a sales process, for example) and then proceed to grind through the details until we sort of stumble over the finish line. What happens next? "OK. Got that done. Now what? Oh, I guess we just do that all over again with the next customer, huh?"

That, my friends, is a recipe for burnout. What I just described was the grind. And it's not healthy in the long run.

But if we see the end as the celebration of the sale and if we begin with the end in mind, we find an interesting psychological hack. We can train our brains to look for the benefits of a job well done.

If you are in sales this is very simple. Just set up a reward system that is commensurate with the effort it took to accomplish your goals.

It might look something like this: "I'm gonna make myself a deal. When I get a sale, I'm gonna take my significant other out to dinner. Every time I get a sale, we're gonna celebrate with a nice dinner. That's my new rule."

If you're more ambitious it might look like this: "If I exceed my sales goal by 20% for the entire year, we're going to Europe for two weeks."

My wife and I did this several years ago. We had the airline miles so we knew we were going to Europe. We determined the quality of the trip based on the business results in the six months preceding the vacation. If we had a horrible half-year we would still go to Europe, but we would stay in hostels and eat Top Ramen in our room. If we had a decent six months we would stay in mid-range hotels and splurge every now and then. And if we had a stellar six months we would stay at the Four Seasons and eat in all the best restaurants. I cannot begin to tell you how motivating that was!

What would really motivate you as a reward for your success? A new boat, perhaps? New wheels? A dream vacation? A new pool in the backyard?

Planning the celebration helps you achieve your goals. Here's why:

A numeric goal is an abstract. To say, "I'm going to sell X number of units," is nothing more than a concept. To some extent, a financial goal is likewise nothing more than a mental construct. "I'm going to make X dollars in commissions this year." That's nice, but it's purely conceptual.

But dinner or a European vacation or a new pool—these things are not abstract; they are concrete. Your mind can quickly understand that these results will get you those rewards.

Make the goal commensurate with the size of the achievement.

Small achievement = modest goal.

Huge achievement = grand goal.

The idea here is to set this up in advance. Let the goal dictate the necessary steps to get there.

Want to really have some fun with this? Plan the celebration with someone else—a family member or friend. Make those people the beneficiaries of your hard work.

Over and over again when we think about execution we think

only about getting the job done. We're missing a step. I want you thinking about how you reward yourself when you get the job done.

Take that time to celebrate your wins and plan that celebration in advance. It will make a huge motivational difference.

Celebrate your victories and you'll execute flawlessly.

My challenge for you

What *really* motivates you? This week I challenge you to begin your week with your end goal in mind. How many sales are you going to close and how will you celebrate your success?

Do it! Make a plan. Today!

SELF-STUDY QUESTIONS:

1. *When is the last time you rewarded yourself for getting a sale? How did it make you feel?*

2. *Visualize what you consider to be a successful quarter of sales. What will you have accomplished at the end of the quarter? How many sales will you have made or how much commission? Now, write down your goal and identify what you will do to celebrate your success.*

3. *How will your incorporate your family, friends, and maybe even your colleagues into your victories?*

. . . .

. . . .

. . . .

. . . .

. . . .

. . . .

. . . .

. . . .

. . . .

. . . .

. . . .

Don't Let Your Team Settle For "Good Enough"!

ORDER A BUNDLE OF 10 AND SAVE

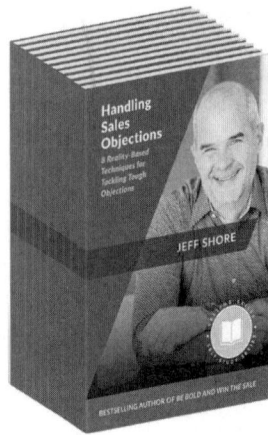

Handling Sales Objections

*The Keys to Unstoppable
Sales Success*

*Dealing with Challenging
Customers in Sales*

FREE BONUS GIFT:
Order now and you'll receive an instant bonus:
JEFF'S SALES TRAINING VIDEO SERIES
visit **shop.jeffshore.com**